a little book of

hugs™

for

Women

D0971252

ISBN: 0-7407-1186-5

Library of Congress Catalog Card Number: 00-102162

Messages by Caron Loveless
Personalized Scriptures by LeAnn Weiss
Interior design by LinDee Loveland and Vanessa Bearden
Project Editor: Philis Boultinghouse

Contents

A WOMAN'S *Touch* 1

A WOMAN'S *Potential* . . . 15

A WOMAN'S *Creativity* . . 29

A WOMAN'S *Thanks* 43

A WOMAN'S *Worth* 59

Remember the
wonderful blessings that
come to you each day from
the hands of a generous
and gracious God, and
forget the irritations that
would detract from your
happiness.

William Arthur Ward

A WOMAN'S

Touch

1

You are a special and needed part of the body of Christ. Even if you feel weak or insignificant, you are indispensable! I've shaped you with special gifts of service needed for

the common good.
I've arranged you
and gifted you to be
needed.

Love,

YOUR GOD
AND CREATOR

1 Corinthians 12

Without women, the whole world would be void of color. As far as the eye could see, all would be brown, flat black, flannel gray, and metal chrome.

There would be no need for bright fuchsia flip-flops, pastel Post-it notes, or Perfectly Pink lipstick. Why, without women, who would point out the sunsets or paint a guest room periwinkle blue?

5 *Touch*

Without women in the world, all the lawns would look just alike: flat, boring grass and a tightly trimmed hedge.

Who would plant
petunias by the fence or
impatiens under the trees
or put daisies in a pot on
the porch? Without
women, there would be
no jasmine on warm
summer nights or roses
to grace your table.

7

Touch

If all the women were gone, the whole wide world would be cold and staid and serious. There would be no giggling or sidesplitting laughter, no more surprise parties or spontaneous songs.

Yes, there would still be old silver spoons, but who would stop to collect them and mount them in eye-pleasing fashion? Without women, who would suggest picnics in the park or dances after dark? And who in the world would snap the family photographs?

9 *Touch*

*O*ne thing is sure: If all the women were gone, the global economy would collapse. There would be no need for shopping malls and department stores; Wal-Mart would stand deserted. Billions of people would have no work; once-happy folk would starve and roam homeless.

$\mathcal{B}$ut this may be the very worst of all—if there were no more women on earth, who would kiss the newborn's cheeks or rock a baby when he cries or sing that child to sleep?

11 $\mathcal{T}$ouch

Look for a reason to need people, and they will need you in return.

M. Norvel Young

A WOMAN'S

Potential

15

*My daughter,
you are My work-
manship, created in
Christ Jesus to do
good works. I've
already prepared*

you in advance for everything I've planned especially for you to do.

Love,

YOUR GOD
OF PURPOSE

Ephesians 2:10

A Woman's

You look inside and
see the unfinished project
that is your life, but do
you know what God sees?

18

God sees the untapped
potential that trickles
deep within you like a
stream on the floor of an
ice-bound river.

Potential

When you see yourself as insecure, God doesn't. He sees a woman with a rich capacity for empathy.

And when you stare into the mirror of imperfection, God sees the etchings of His artistry—designs He drew so that you could be *you*.

When you look around
and see a roadblock in
your path, God sees all the
interesting side roads you
could take to get around it.

When you see all the
people who never fail to
depend on you, God sees
all the lives that are
blessed by you.

Potential

21

A Woman's

When you see a
thankless routine, God
sees the fruit of your
faithful life.

When you see lost
relationships, God sees
room for new friends.

*W*hen you see tangled complications, God sees a place for a miracle.

When you see loneliness and abandonment, God sees the gaping hole in your heart and knows that only He can fill it.

Potential

A Woman's

*W*hen you see a past-empty bank account, God sees the perfect chance for His cherished child to watch how He'll provide.

When you see truckloads of stress begin to roll your way, God sees emerald-green pastures beside crystal-clear waters and makes His plans to take you there for refreshment.

And when the days
come that all you can see
is darkness and gloom,
God sees only the bright,
new hope shining on your
horizon—and He smiles,
for He knows the endless
joys that a future with
Him will bring to you.

Potential

Depending upon him
alone,
I go forward…though my
eyes are wet with tears, I
must go forward. O
Lord, fill me with the
Holy Ghost. Give me
power to move the people.
Amen.

Kiye Sato Yamamuro

A
WOMAN'S

Creativity

Celebrate

your uniqueness!
No one else can do
what I've created
you to do! Use the
special gifts and
abilities I have
given you to serve

others and to faith-
fully administer
My amazing grace
as only you can.

Love,

YOUR LORD
OF CREATIVITY

1 Peter 4:10

Because she was made
in the likeness of God, a
woman is born to create.
From her amazing *hands,*
a mound of sticky dough
becomes a slice of bread, a
piece of silken cloth
becomes an evening dress,
and a rocky patch of
ground yields fruit.

*F*rom the work of a woman's hands, a tired antique is reborn, a faded couch is recovered, and a clump of gathered blooms becomes a bride's bouquet.

Creativity

Because she is made
in God's image, there are
gifts in a woman's hands
—gifts whose cost is time,
gifts that are tiny tidbits
of herself, showered over
her neighbors, family, and
friends.

She makes gifts to cheer, to celebrate, and to share—creations from her heart, just because she cares.

Her creativity fuels a life of love and giving.

Creativity

A woman is born to
create, and out of her
heart flow passions to
make pictures with pencils
or paint, to orchestrate
outstanding performances,
to turn a plain kitchen
table into an elegant feast.

When a woman puts her heart into it, mere cookies become tender offerings, scrapbooks are transformed into heirlooms, and an old spotted sheet is quickly converted into a costume.

Creativity

Because she was made
in the image of God, a
woman has a *head* for
the harmonious.

　　She can dance her way
through disputes, work to
troubleshoot conflicts, and
help others solve their
problems.

A woman is a thinker,
a dreamer, a weaver of tales,
a poet, a prophet, and a
princess.

And because she was
made in the image of God,
the thoughts in her *head,*
the love in her *heart,*
and the work of her *hands*
have been blessed.

Creativity

*We are each inspired
treasures, with creative gifts
to share. The world needs
your gifts!*

Sark

A WOMAN'S

Thanks

You can do it! It's not always easy, but remember, you're not alone. You have an unlimited power source supporting you.

You can do all things because I strengthen you!

Love,

THE LORD
YOUR HELPER

Philippians 4:13

To the Women Who
Have Touched My Life:

Once upon a time, you
noticed me and welcomed
me into your life. You made
me feel special, valuable,
and likeable—and for that
gift, I will be forever grateful.

It was you who first saw potential in me; and while others were silent on the subject, you blabbed my best features to the world. With loving arms, you enfolded me and taught my heart about hope. You showed my eyes how to see, told my ears how to hear, and taught my feet where to walk.

Thanks

All those times I poured out my heart and spoke my mind, you sat there, patiently listening. You let me be me; but all the time, I was longing to be you. I made a study of your life.

I weighed your words.
I copied your clothes. I
wanted to carry myself with
your confidence, intelligence,
and faith. I watched for the
secrets of your success. You
gave me a star to shoot for, a
standard to live by.

Thanks

More than anything else, I hoped I could make your heart proud. I may not leap tall buildings in a single bound, but thanks to you, I am not afraid to try. Because of you, I know the meaning of *grace*.

Because of you, I am
confident enough to say
that there is a better day
on the way, even when I
cannot see it.

Thanks

*F*or knowing you, I am far richer, wiser, and happier than I ever could have been on my own. Once upon a time, I tasted your life; and to this day, it feeds my soul.

I just wanted to let you know that. I just wanted to give you my thanks.

Thanks

A nation is not
conquered until the
hearts of its women are
on the ground.
Then it is done, no matter
how brave its warriors
nor how strong their
weapons.

Cheyenne Proverb

They talk about a woman's sphere
As though it had a limit;
There's not a task
to mankind given,
There's not a blessing or a woe,
There's not a whispered
"yes" or "no,"
There's not a life,
there's not a birth
That has a feather's weight
of worth
Without a woman in it.

Speaker's Sourcebook

A
WOMAN'S

Worth

You are loved! Sometimes in the midst of trials, you will feel unloved, unappreciated, alone, and abandoned. Even then, know that I am still working and will fulfill My special purpose for you. I'm right there to preserve your life and help you.

My love for you lasts forever! Nothing and no one in this universe could ever stop Me from loving you.

Love,

YOUR GOD
AND CREATOR

Psalm 138:7–8; Romans 8:38–39

*S*hould the day come that the whole wide world knows your name due to some monumental achievement and they ride you through the streets in an open convertible as people shout and cheer and throw confetti from high-rise office buildings—of course, God will be proud of your success…

But He will not love
you one ounce more than
He does at this moment.
It's just not possible.

Worth

Or should the day
come that you lose
your "golden touch"
and the thing you have
been good at all your
life begins to fail you—
God will understand…

But He will not
flinch or bat an eye,
because His love for you
transcends all failure.

Worth

*O*r should a time come
that you decide to sell
your earthly possessions
and devote the rest of
your life to healing the
sick in some foreign
land—God will smile…

*B*ut He will also keep
on loving you with the
same degree of intensity
He always has. That's a
fact.

Worth

*O*r if the time comes
that you embarrass yourself
and everyone present by
losing your cool and
blurting out angry, hurtful
words in a public place—
God will be saddened…

*B*ut not one tiny speck
of His affection for you will
be altered.

You see, long, long ago
God made up His heart
about you, and when God
makes up His heart to love
someone, there is absolutely,
positively nothing you can
ever do to change it.

*To love and be loved is to
feel the sun from both sides.*

Barbara Johnson

Look for these other little *Hugs* books:
A Little Book of Hugs for Friends
A Little Book of Hugs for Mom
A Little Book of Hugs for Sisters
A Little Book of Hugs for Teachers
A Little Book of Hugs to Encourage and Inspire

Also look for these full-size *Hugs* books:
Hugs for Women
Hugs for Friends
Hugs for Mom
Hugs for Kids
Hugs for Teachers
Hugs for Sisters
Hugs for Those in Love
Hugs for the Hurting
Hugs for Grandparents
Hugs for Dad
Hugs for the Holidays
Hugs to Encourage and Inspire